Life Lessons

from THE INSPIRED WORD of GOD

BOOK of JAMES

MAX LUCADO

General Editor

LIFE LESSONS FROM THE INSPIRED WORD OF GOD—BOOK OF JAMES

Scripture passages taken from:

The Holy Bible, *New Century Version*
Copyright ©1987, 1988, 1991 by Word Publishing. All rights reserved.

The Holy Bible, *New King James Version*
Copyright © 1979, 1980, 1982 by Thomas Nelson. All rights reserved.

All excerpts used by permission.

Design and cover art—by Koechel Peterson and Associates, Inc., Minneapolis, Minnesota.

Produced with the assistance of the Livingstone Corporation.

ISBN: 08499-5248-4
Published by Word Publishing

TABLE OF CONTENTS

HOW TO STUDY THE BIBLE

BY MAX LUCADO

*T*his is a peculiar book you are holding. Words crafted in another language. Deeds done in a distant era. Events recorded in a far-off land. Counsel offered to a foreign people. This is a peculiar book.

It's surprising that anyone reads it. It's too old. Some of its writings date back five thousand years. It's too bizarre. The book speaks of incredible floods, fires, earthquakes, and people with supernatural abilities. It's too radical. The Bible calls for undying devotion to a carpenter who called himself God's Son.

Logic says this book shouldn't survive. Too old, too bizarre, too radical.

The Bible has been banned, burned, scoffed, and ridiculed. Scholars have mocked it as foolish. Kings have branded it as illegal. A thousand times over it the grave has been dug and the dirge has begun, but somehow the Bible never stays in the grave. Not only has it survived, it has thrived. It is the single most popular book in all of history. It has been the best-selling book in the world for years!

There is no way on earth to explain it. Which perhaps is the only explanation. The answer? The Bible's durability is not found on earth; it is found in heaven. For the millions who have tested its claims and claimed its promises, there is but one answer—the Bible is God's book and God's voice.

As you read it, you would be wise to give some thought to two questions. What is the purpose of the Bible? and How do I study the Bible? Time spent reflecting on these two issues will greatly enhance your Bible study.

What is the purpose of the Bible?

Let the Bible itself answer that question.

Since you were a child you have known the Holy Scriptures which are able to make you wise. And that wisdom leads to salvation through faith in Christ Jesus.

(2 Tim. 3:15)

The purpose of the Bible? Salvation. God's highest passion is to get his children home. His book, the Bible, describes his plan of salvation. The purpose of the Bible is to proclaim God's plan and passion to save his children.

That is the reason this book has endured through the centuries. It dares to tackle the toughest questions about life: Where do I go after I die? Is there a God? What do I do with my fears? The Bible offers answers to these crucial questions. It is the treasure map that leads us to God's highest treasure, eternal life.

But how do we use the Bible? Countless copies of Scripture sit unread on bookshelves and nightstands simply because people don't know how to read it. What can we do to make the Bible real in our lives?

The clearest answer is found in the words of Jesus.

"Ask," he promised, *"and God will give it to you. Search and you will find. Knock, and the door will open for you."*

(Matt. 7:7)

The first step in understanding the Bible is asking God to help us. We should read prayerfully. If anyone understands God's Word, it is because of God and not the reader.

But the Helper will teach you everything and will cause you to remember all that I told you. The Helper is the Holy Spirit whom the Father will send in my name.

(John 14:24)

Before reading the Bible, pray. Invite God to speak to you. Don't go to Scripture looking for your idea, go searching for his.

Not only should we read the Bible prayerfully, we should read it carefully. *Search and you will find* is the pledge. The Bible is not a newspaper to be skimmed but rather a mine to be quarried. *Search for it like silver, and hunt for it like hidden treasure. Then you will understand respect for the LORD, and you will find that you know God* (Prov. 2:4).

Any worthy find requires effort. The Bible is no exception. To understand the Bible you don't have to be brilliant, but you must be willing to roll up your sleeves and search.

Be a worker who is not ashamed and who uses the true teaching in the right way.

(2 Tim. 2:15)

Here's a practical point. Study the Bible a bit at a time. Hunger is not satisfied by eating twenty-one meals in one sitting once a week. The body needs a steady diet to remain strong. So does the soul. When God sent food to his people in the wilderness, he didn't provide loaves already made. Instead, he sent them manna in the shape of *thin flakes, like frost . . . on the desert ground* (Exod. 16:14).

God gave manna in limited portions.

God sends spiritual food the same way. He opens the heavens with just enough nutrients for today's hunger. He provides, *a command here, a command there. A rule here, a rule there. A little lesson here, a little lesson there* (Isa. 28:10).

Don't be discouraged if your reading reaps a small harvest. Some days a lesser portion is all that is needed. What is important is to search every day for that day's message. A steady diet of God's Word over a lifetime builds a healthy soul and mind.

A little girl returned from her first day at school. Her mom asked, "Did you learn anything?" "Apparently not enough," the girl responded, "I have to go back tomorrow and the next day and the next. . . ."

Such is the case with learning. And such is the case with Bible study. Understanding comes little by little over a lifetime.

There is a third step in understanding the Bible. After the asking and seeking comes the knocking. After you ask and search, then knock.

Knock, and the door will open for you.
(Matt. 7:7)

To knock is to stand at God's door. To make yourself available. To climb the steps, cross the porch, stand at the doorway, and volunteer. Knocking goes beyond the realm of thinking and into the realm of acting.

To knock is to ask, What can I do? How can I obey? Where can I go?

It's one thing to know what to do. It's another to do it. But for those who do it, those who choose to obey, a special reward awaits them.

The truly happy are those who carefully study God's perfect law that makes people free, and they continue to study it. They do not forget what they heard, but they obey what God's teaching says. Those who do this will be made happy.
(James 1:25)

What a promise. Happiness comes to those who do what they read! It's the same with medicine. If you only read the label but ignore the pills, it won't help. It's the same with food. If you only read the recipe but never cook, you won't be fed. And it's the same with the Bible. If you only read the words but never obey, you'll never know the joy God has promised.

Ask. Search. Knock. Simple, isn't it? Why don't you give it a try? If you do, you'll see why you are holding the most remarkable book in history.

INTRODUCTION

*H*ere is a story James would have liked. Francis of Assisi once invited an apprentice to go with him to a nearby village to preach. The young monk quickly agreed, seizing an opportunity to hear his teacher speak. When they arrived in the village, St. Francis began to visit with the people.

First he stopped in on the butcher. Next a visit with the cobbler. Then a short walk to the home of a woman who'd recently buried her husband. After that a stop at the school to chat with the teacher. This continued throughout the morning. After some time, Francis told his disciple that it was time to return to the abbey.

The student didn't understand. "But we came to preach," he reminded. "We haven't preached a sermon."

"Haven't we?" questioned the elder. "People have watched us, listened to us, responded to us. Every word we have spoken, every deed we have done has been a sermon. We have preached all morning."

James would have liked that. As far as he was concerned, Christianity was more action on Monday than worship on Sunday. "My brothers and sisters, if people say they have faith but do nothing, their faith is worth nothing. Can faith like that save them?" (2:14).

His message is bare-knuckled; his style is bare-boned. Talk is cheap, he argues. Service is invaluable.

It's not that works save the Christian, but that works mark the Christian. In James's book of logic, it only makes sense that we who have been given much should give much. Not just with words. But with our lives.

Or as St. Francis is noted as saying, "Preach without ceasing. If you must, use words."

James would have liked that, too.

LESSON ONE

GROWING THROUGH TRIALS

REFLECTION

Begin your study by sharing thoughts on this question.

1. Think of a recent problem or difficulty in your life. In what ways did God give you strength to face that situation?

_____

_____

_____

BIBLE READING

Read James 1:1–11 from the NCV or the NKJV.

N C V

¹From James, a servant of God and of the Lord Jesus Christ.

To all of God's people who are scattered everywhere in the world:

Greetings.

²My brothers and sisters, when you have many kinds of troubles, you should be full of joy, ³because you know that these troubles test your faith, and this will give you patience. ⁴Let

N K J V

¹James, a bondservant of God and of the Lord Jesus Christ,

To the twelve tribes which are scattered abroad:

Greetings.

²My brethren, count it all joy when you fall into various trials, ³knowing that the testing of your faith produces patience. ⁴But let patience have its perfect work, that you may be perfect

NCV

your patience show itself perfectly in what you do. Then you will be perfect and complete and will have everything you need. ⁵But if any of you needs wisdom, you should ask God for it. He is generous and enjoys giving to all people, so he will give you wisdom. ⁶But when you ask God, you must believe and not doubt. Anyone who doubts is like a wave in the sea, blown up and down by the wind. ⁷⁻⁸Such doubters are thinking two different things at the same time, and they cannot decide about anything they do. They should not think they will receive anything from the Lord.

⁹Believers who are poor should be proud, because God has made them spiritually rich. ¹⁰Those who are rich should be proud, because God has shown them that they are spiritually poor. The rich will die like a wild flower in the grass. ¹¹The sun rises with burning heat and dries up the plants. The flower falls off, and its beauty is gone. In the same way the rich will die while they are still taking care of business.

NKJV

and complete, lacking nothing. ⁵If any of you lacks wisdom, let him ask of God, who gives to all liberally and without reproach, and it will be given to him. ⁶But let him ask in faith, with no doubting, for he who doubts is like a wave of the sea driven and tossed by the wind. ⁷For let not that man suppose that he will receive anything from the Lord; ⁸he is a double-minded man, unstable in all his ways.

⁹Let the lowly brother glory in his exaltation, ¹⁰but the rich in his humiliation, because as a flower of the field he will pass away. ¹¹For no sooner has the sun risen with a burning heat than it withers the grass; its flower falls, and its beautiful appearance perishes. So the rich man also will fade away in his pursuits.

DISCOVERY

Explore the Bible reading by discussing these questions.

2. How does Scripture encourage people to respond to trials?

_____

_____

_____

3. How has God brought good into your life through trials?

_____

_____

_____

4. How can a person gain wisdom to deal with problems?

_____

_____

_____

5. Why does God want us to ask for his help without doubting?

_____

_____

_____

6. Who should not expect to receive anything from God? Why?

_____

_____

_____

INSPIRATION

Here is an uplifting thought from the *Inspirational Study Bible.*

When a potter bakes a pot, he checks its solidity by pulling it out of the oven and thumping it. If it "sings," it's ready. If it "thuds," it's placed back in the oven. The character of a person is also checked by thumping.

Been thumped lately?

Late-night phone calls. Grouchy teacher. Grumpy moms. Burnt meals. Flat tires. "You've got to be kidding" deadlines. Those are thumps. Thumps are those irritating inconveniences that trigger the worst in us. They catch us off guard. Flat footed. They aren't big enough to be crises, but if you get enough of them, watch out! Traffic jams. Long lines. Empty mailboxes. Dirty clothes on the floor . . . Thump. Thump. Thump. How do I respond? Do I sing? Or do I thud? Jesus said that out of the nature of the heart a man speaks (Luke 6:45). There's nothing like a good thump to reveal the nature of a heart. The true character of a person is seen not in momentary heroics, but in the thump-packed humdrum of day-to-day living.

(from *On the Anvil*
by Max Lucado)

RESPONSE

Use these questions to share more deeply with each other.

7. How have life's "thumps" challenged you to seek God?

_____

_____

_____

8. How has your relationship with God changed as you have gone through trials and difficulties?

_____

_____

_____

9. In what ways does this passage relate to your present problems and frustrations?

_____

_____

_____

PRAYER

Father, we come to you just as we are, struggling to cope with the trials of life. We're grateful that you never turn your back on us. You promise to give us the wisdom and strength we need to face each day. Continue to test us until our character shines and brings glory to you.

JOURNALING

Take a few moments to record your personal insights from this lesson.

How can I grow closer to God through trials I am facing now?

ADDITIONAL QUESTIONS

10. How do you usually respond to life's difficulties?

_____

_____

_____

11. How can you find joy in your troubles?

_____

_____

_____

12. Describe a time when God's wisdom helped you through a problem.

_____

_____

_____

For more Bible passages on growing through trials, see Romans 5:3, 4;
2 Corinthians 4:17; 6:4; 2 Thessalonians 1:4; 1 Peter 1:5–7; 4:12–14.

To complete the book of James during this twelve-part study, read James 1:1–11.

ADDITIONAL THOUGHTS

LESSON TWO

ENDURING TEMPTATION

REFLECTION

Begin your study by sharing thoughts on this question.

1. In what ways have you received good gifts from God?

_____

_____

_____

BIBLE READING

Read James 1:12–18 from the NCV or the NKJV.

NCV

¹²When people are tempted and still continue strong, they should be happy. After they have proved their faith, God will reward them with life forever. God promised this to all those who love him. ¹³When people are tempted, they should not say, "God is tempting me." Evil cannot tempt God, and God himself does not tempt anyone. ¹⁴But people are tempted when their own evil desire leads them away and traps them. ¹⁵This desire leads to sin, and then the sin grows and brings death.

NKJV

¹²Blessed is the man who endures temptation; for when he has been approved, he will receive the crown of life which the Lord has promised to those who love Him. ¹³Let no one say when he is tempted, "I am tempted by God"; for God cannot be tempted by evil, nor does He Himself tempt anyone. ¹⁴But each one is tempted when he is drawn away by his own desires and enticed. ¹⁵Then, when desire has conceived, it gives birth to sin; and sin, when it is full-grown, brings forth death.

NCV

[16]My dear brothers and sisters, do not be fooled about this. [17]Every good action and every perfect gift is from God. These good gifts come down from the Creator of the sun, moon, and stars, who does not change like their shifting shadows. [18]God decided to give us life through the word of truth so we might be the most important of all the things he made.

NKJV

[16]Do not be deceived, my beloved brethren. [17]Every good gift and every perfect gift is from above, and comes down from the Father of lights, with whom there is no variation or shadow of turning. [18]Of His own will He brought us forth by the word of truth, that we might be a kind of firstfruits of His creatures.

DISCOVERY

Explore the Bible reading by discussing these questions.

2. How can we remain strong to resist temptation?

_____

_____

_____

3. How does God reward faithful people?

_____

_____

_____

4. Who do some people blame as the source of temptation? Why?

_____

_____

_____

5. Why are we tempted?

_____

_____

_____

6. List the results of continually giving in to sin.

_____

_____

_____

INSPIRATION

Here is an uplifting thought from the *Inspirational Study Bible.*

So there are external spiritual forces which are at work in this world, seeking to keep us from God and His will. . . .

And this is not just external to us. This battle goes on inside of us. . . . Maybe your sin is wrong sexual desires, pride, gluttony, laziness, or anger, or some other besetting sin. . . . But you feel the inner struggle. Sometimes you conclude just as Paul did in Romans 7:22–24 ["What a struggle!"]

But don't stop there! Note Paul's glorious conclusion in verse 25 and 8:2. . . . "Thanks be to God through Jesus Christ our Lord! . . . For the law of the Spirit of life in Christ Jesus has set you free from the law of sin and death."

(from *The Holy Spirit* by Billy Graham)

RESPONSE

Use these questions to share more deeply with each other.

7. List new insights from this passage about temptation.

_____

_____

_____

8. How has the testimony of others helped you in your struggle against sin?

_____

_____

_____

9. How can you encourage others to resist temptation?

_____

_____

_____

PRAYER

Father, when we confront temptation, we pray that you would give us strength to resist evil. Thank you for your promise that if we do what is right, eventually truth, justice, and goodness will prevail.

JOURNALING

Take a few moments to record your personal insights from this lesson.

How has God set me free from sin and temptation?

ADDITIONAL QUESTIONS

10. What temptations are most difficult for you to resist?

_____

_____

_____

11. How can you resist those temptations?

_____

_____

_____

12. List how you can depend more on God for the strength to overcome sin.

_____

_____

_____

For more Bible passages on temptation, see Matthew 6:13; 26:41; Luke 4:1, 2; Romans 8:5–8; 1 Corinthians 10:13; Galatians 6:1; Ephesians 6:11–13; Hebrews 4:15, 16.

To complete the book of James during this twelve-part study, read James 1:12–18.

LESSON THREE

LIVING PROOF

REFLECTION

Begin your study by sharing thoughts on this question.

1. Think of one person who truly exemplifies godliness. How has that person's life been an example to you?

_____

_____

_____

BIBLE READING

Read James 1:19–27 from the NCV or the NKJV.

NCV

19My dear brothers and sisters, always be willing to listen and slow to speak. Do not become angry easily, 20because anger will not help you live the right kind of life God wants. 21So put out of your life every evil thing and every kind of wrong. Then in gentleness accept God's teaching that is planted in your hearts, which can save you.

22Do what God's teaching says; when you only listen and do nothing, you are fooling

NKJV

19So then, my beloved brethren, let every man be swift to hear, slow to speak, slow to wrath; 20for the wrath of man does not produce the righteousness of God.

21Therefore lay aside all filthiness and overflow of wickedness, and receive with meekness the implanted word, which is able to save your souls.

22But be doers of the word, and not hearers only, deceiving yourselves. 23For if anyone is a

NCV

yourselves. ²³Those who hear God's teaching and do nothing are like people who look at themselves in a mirror. ²⁴They see their faces and then go away and quickly forget what they looked like. ²⁵But the truly happy people are those who carefully study God's perfect law that makes people free, and they continue to study it. They do not forget what they heard, but they obey what God's teaching says. Those who do this will be made happy.

²⁶People who think they are religious but say things they should not say are just fooling themselves. Their "religion" is worth nothing. ²⁷Religion that God accepts as pure and without fault is this: caring for orphans or widows who need help, and keeping yourself free from the world's evil influence.

NKJV

hearer of the word and not a doer, he is like a man observing his natural face in a mirror; ²⁴for he observes himself, goes away, and immediately forgets what kind of man he was. ²⁵But he who looks into the perfect law of liberty and continues in it, and is not a forgetful hearer but a doer of the work, this one will be blessed in what he does.

²⁶If anyone among you thinks he is religious, and does not bridle his tongue but deceives his own heart, this one's religion is useless. ²⁷Pure and undefiled religion before God and the Father is this: to visit orphans and widows in their trouble, and to keep oneself unspotted from the world.

DISCOVERY

Explore the Bible reading by discussing these questions.

2. How does this passage describe living a good life?

_____

_____

_____

3. List some of the ways people can deceive themselves.

_____

_____

_____

4. How does this passage describe people who do not obey God's word?

_____

_____

_____

5. How does God bless those who study and obey his Word?

_____

_____

_____

6. How can you practice "pure and undefiled religion"?

_____

_____

_____

INSPIRATION

Here is an uplifting thought from the *Inspirational Study Bible.*

According to Gallup surveys, confirmed by other polls taken over the past fifteen years, 33 percent of all Americans over age eighteen indicate they are evangelical or "born again" Christians. That translates into 59 million Christians, or one in every three adults, who experienced a turning point in their lives as they made a personal commitment to Jesus Christ.

This information should grip us with terror. It means that the greatest revival in history has so far been impotent to change society. It's *revival* without *reformation*. It's a revival which left the country floundering in spiritual ignorance. It's a change in *belief* without a corresponding change in *behavior*. . . .

How did the building blocks of the gospel become glued together with the cement of self-centeredness? The American gospel has evolved into a gospel of addition without subtraction. It is the belief that we can add Christ to our lives, but not subtract sin. It is a change in belief without a change in behavior. It is a spiritual experience without any cultural impact. It is revival without reformation, without repentance. . . .

The *proof* of religious conversion is to demonstrate that we have both added a relationship with Christ and that we have subtracted sin (repentance). And we multiply proof to a weary world by what we do—our deeds, our obedience. What we do must confirm what we say. Our deeds are the proof of our repentance. . . .

A changed life is one that has added Christ and subtracted sin, that attracts a world weary of worn-out words. Obedience is the proof.

(from *Walking with Christ in the Details of Life* by Patrick Morley)

RESPONSE

Use these questions to share more deeply with each other.

7. In what ways should a person's life change after conversion?

_____

_____

_____

8. How does the world pressure us to disobey God's Word?

_____

_____

_____

9. List some practical ways to protect yourself from the world's influence.

_____

_____

_____

PRAYER

Father, help us to hear your voice amidst the manifold voices of the world. Help us to put into practice the timeless truths found in your Word. Most of all, Father, help us remember that you have set us free—free from the lures of this world. Thank you for your promise that when the Son sets us free, we are free indeed.

JOURNALING

Take a few moments to record your personal insights from this lesson.

How does God help me remove sin from my life?

ADDITIONAL QUESTIONS

10. In what ways has your life changed since your conversion?

_____

_____

_____

11. Why do we sometimes find it difficult to do what we know is right?

_____

_____

_____

12. In what ways does your life demonstrate to others that you are a Christian?

_____

_____

_____

For more Bible passages on obedience, see Leviticus 19:2; Acts 5:29; Romans 6; 2 Corinthians 7:1; 9:13; Titus 3:1; Hebrews 12:13, 14; 1 Peter 1:14; 1 John 3:24; 2 John 6.

To complete the book of James during this twelve-part study, read James 1:19–27.

ADDITIONAL THOUGHTS

LESSON FOUR

EQUALITY IN THE CHURCH

REFLECTION

Begin your study by sharing thoughts on this question.

1. When people visit your church, how do you make them feel welcome?

_____

_____

_____

BIBLE READING

Read James 2:1–13 from the NCV or the NKJV.

NCV

¹My dear brothers and sisters, as believers in our glorious Lord Jesus Christ, never think some people are more important than others. ²Suppose someone comes into your church meeting wearing nice clothes and a gold ring. At the same time a poor person comes in wearing old, dirty clothes. ³You show special attention to the one wearing nice clothes and say, "Please, sit here in this good seat." But you say to the poor person, "Stand over there," or, "Sit on the floor by my feet." ⁴What are you doing? You are making some people more important

NKJV

¹My brethren, do not hold the faith of our Lord Jesus Christ, the Lord of glory, with partiality. ²For if there should come into your assembly a man with gold rings, in fine apparel, and there should also come in a poor man in filthy clothes, ³and you pay attention to the one wearing the fine clothes and say to him, "You sit here in a good place," and say to the poor man, "You stand there," or, "Sit here at my footstool," ⁴have you not shown partiality among yourselves, and become judges with evil thoughts?

NCV

than others, and with evil thoughts you are deciding that one person is better.

⁵Listen, my dear brothers and sisters! God chose the poor in the world to be rich with faith and to receive the kingdom God promised to those who love him. ⁶But you show no respect to the poor. The rich are always trying to control your lives. They are the ones who take you to court. ⁷And they are the ones who speak against Jesus, who owns you.

⁸This royal law is found in the Scriptures: "Love your neighbor as you love yourself." If you obey this law, you are doing right. ⁹But if you treat one person as being more important than another, you are sinning. You are guilty of breaking God's law. ¹⁰A person who follows all of God's law but fails to obey even one command is guilty of breaking all the commands in that law. ¹¹The same God who said, "You must not be guilty of adultery," also said, "You must not murder anyone." So if you do not take part in adultery but you murder someone, you are guilty of breaking all of God's law. ¹²In everything you say and do, remember that you will be judged by the law that makes people free. ¹³So you must show mercy to others, or God will not show mercy to you when he judges you. But the person who shows mercy can stand without fear at the judgment.

NKJV

⁵Listen, my beloved brethren: Has God not chosen the poor of this world to be rich in faith and heirs of the kingdom which He promised to those who love Him? ⁶But you have dishonored the poor man. Do not the rich oppress you and drag you into the courts? ⁷Do they not blaspheme that noble name by which you are called?

⁸If you really fulfill the royal law according to the Scripture, "You shall love your neighbor as yourself," you do well; ⁹but if you show partiality, you commit sin, and are convicted by the law as transgressors. ¹⁰For whoever shall keep the whole law, and yet stumble in one point, he is guilty of all. ¹¹For He who said, "Do not commit adultery," also said, "Do not murder." Now if you do not commit adultery, but you do murder, you have become a transgressor of the law. ¹²So speak and so do as those who will be judged by the law of liberty. ¹³For judgment is without mercy to the one who has shown no mercy. Mercy triumphs over judgment.

DISCOVERY

Explore the Bible reading by discussing these questions.

2. Why is it wrong to treat rich people better than poor people?

_____

_____

_____

3. How does God treat the poor and powerless?

_____

_____

_____

4. Explain how partiality makes us unjust judges.

_____

_____

_____

5. How does showing favoritism indicate a feeling of superiority?

_____

_____

_____

6. List how Christians can show mercy.

_____

_____

_____

INSPIRATION

Here is an uplifting thought from the *Inspirational Study Bible.*

Grant's church was beginning a ministry to people suffering from AIDS. At the initial planning session, an expert on this type of ministry was going to be present to speak to the group about the *Dos* and *Don'ts* of such a task. The catch was that the person who was coming had AIDS.

As he drove to the meeting, Grant struggled with what his response would be. "How should I address this individual? Would I shake hands with this person? Would I sit next to him? Would I pry into his lifestyle, demanding to know how he contracted the disease? How would I react if he volunteered that information? Is this a ministry that I should be involved in personally?" These questions and countless others were swirling through his mind.

As he pondered these issues, he was reminded of James 2:1 and the fact that favoritism is sin. The issue is not whether the distinction is made over economic, social, educational, physical, spiritual, or health concerns or differences. The issue is that our motives for making the distinction are immediately called into question because favoritism is sin.

(from *A Dad's Blessing*
by Gary Smalley and John Trent)

RESPONSE

Use these questions to share more deeply with each other.

7. List examples of favoritism or prejudice you see in the church today.

_____

_____

_____

8. List some people who might feel uncomfortable in your church.

_____

_____

_____

9. How can your church make those people feel more welcome?

_____

_____

_____

PRAYER

Thank you, Father, that all people are equal in your eyes. Forgive us for judging people by appearances and accomplishments. Forgive us for favoring the rich and powerful over the poor and weak. Oh God, change our hearts. Teach us what it means to love our neighbors as ourselves.

JOURNALING

Take a few moments to record your personal insights from this lesson.

How can I gain victory over the sin of favoritism?

ADDITIONAL QUESTIONS

10. Why do we tend to downplay the seriousness of favoritism?

_____

_____

_____

11. If you have been a victim of favoritism or prejudice, how did it make you feel?

_____

_____

_____

12. How can you help others change their attitudes toward the poor and vulnerable?

_____

_____

_____

For more Bible passages on favoritism, see Exodus 23:2, 3; Leviticus 19:15; Proverbs 19:6; 1 Timothy 5:21.

To complete the book of James during this twelve-part study, read James 2:1–13.

ADDITIONAL THOUGHTS

LESSON FIVE

HOW FAITH WORKS

REFLECTION

Begin your study by sharing thoughts on this question.

1. Think of a time when you saw a group of people rally around someone in need. What motivated the group to help that person?

_____

_____

_____

BIBLE READING

Read James 2:14–26 from the NCV or the NKJV.

NCV

¹⁴My brothers and sisters, if people say they have faith, but do nothing, their faith is worth nothing. Can faith like that save them? ¹⁵A brother or sister in Christ might need clothes or food. ¹⁶If you say to that person, "God be with you! I hope you stay warm and get plenty to eat," but you do not give what that person needs, your words are worth nothing. ¹⁷In the same way, faith that is alone—that does nothing— is dead.

¹⁸Someone might say, "You have faith, but I

NKJV

¹⁴What does it profit, my brethren, if someone says he has faith but does not have works? Can faith save him? ¹⁵If a brother or sister is naked and destitute of daily food, ¹⁶and one of you says to them, "Depart in peace, be warmed and filled," but you do not give them the things which are needed for the body, what does it profit? ¹⁷Thus also faith by itself, if it does not have works, is dead.

¹⁸But someone will say, "You have faith, and I have works." Show me your faith without your

NCV

have deeds." Show me your faith without doing anything, and I will show you my faith by what I do. [19]You believe there is one God. Good! But the demons believe that, too, and they tremble with fear.

[20]You foolish person! Must you be shown that faith that does nothing is worth nothing? [21]Abraham, our ancestor, was made right with God by what he did when he offered his son Isaac on the altar. [22]So you see that Abraham's faith and the things he did worked together. His faith was made perfect by what he did. [23]This shows the full meaning of the Scripture that says: "Abraham believed God, and God accepted Abraham's faith, and that faith made him right with God." And Abraham was called God's friend. [24]So you see that people are made right with God by what they do, not by faith only.

[25]Another example is Rahab, a prostitute, who was made right with God by something she did. She welcomed the spies into her home and helped them escape by a different road. [26]Just as a person's body that does not have a spirit is dead, so faith that does nothing is dead!

NKJV

works, and I will show you my faith by my works. [19]You believe that there is one God. You do well. Even the demons believe—and tremble! [20]But do you want to know, O foolish man, that faith without works is dead? [21]Was not Abraham our father justified by works when he offered Isaac his son on the altar? [22]Do you see that faith was working together with his works, and by works faith was made perfect? [23]And the Scripture was fulfilled which says, "Abraham believed God, and it was accounted to him for righteousness." And he was called the friend of God. [24]You see then that a man is justified by works, and not by faith only.

[25]Likewise, was not Rahab the harlot also justified by works when she received the messengers and sent them out another way?

[26]For as the body without the spirit is dead, so faith without works is dead also.

DISCOVERY

Explore the Bible reading by discussing these questions.

2. Why is faith without works dead?

_____

_____

_____

3. How is living faith demonstrated?

_____

_____

_____

4. How do some people rationalize inactive faith?

_____

_____

_____

5. Explain why mere belief in God is not enough.

_____

_____

_____

6. How did Abraham and Rahab demonstrate their faith?

_____

_____

_____

INSPIRATION

Here is an uplifting thought from the *Inspirational Study Bible*.

"Add to your faith": Supplement it, flesh it out. Being a Christian doesn't mean believing and then just sitting around. Now that you have faith in God's part, make every effort—that's your part.

That's discipline.

That's regular "holy habits."

That's pacing yourself for the cross-country run to your future.

Says Henri Nouwen, "A spiritual life without discipline is impossible." Tighten your belt. Get tough on your self. GO FOR IT.

A woman once said to the great Paderewski, "Sir, you are truly a genius."

"Well," he answered, "before I was a genius, I was a drudge!"

To get there, to win—your life needs discipline, order, and arrangement.

"If one examines the secret behind a championship football team, a magnificent orchestra, or a successful business, the principle ingredient is invariably discipline" (James Dobson, *Discipline of the Home*).

You will only discover excellence on the other side of hard work.

(from *My Sacrifice, His Fire* by Anne Ortlund)

RESPONSE

Use these questions to share more deeply with each other.

7.   What steps can you take to practice true Christianity?

_____

_____

_____

8.   Why is it important to help others?

_____

_____

_____

9. How is helping others part of a disciplined spiritual life?

_____

_____

_____

PRAYER

Father, thank you for your perfect plan of salvation. Thank you for providing a way for us to spend eternity with you. Until then, show us the good work you want us to do, then give us the strength to do it.

JOURNALING

Take a few moments to record your personal insights from this lesson.

How do faith and works go together in my life?

ADDITIONAL QUESTIONS

10. List ways you can reach out to someone in need.

_____

_____

_____

11. How does spiritual discipline help us to practice true Christianity?

_____

_____

_____

12. How can you develop spiritual discipline in your life?

_____

_____

_____

For more Bible passages on faith and works, see John 14:12; Philippians 2:17; 2 Thessalonians 1:11; Hebrews 6:9–12; 2 Peter 1:5–7.

To complete the book of James during this twelve-part study, read James 2:14–26.

ADDITIONAL THOUGHTS

LESSON SIX

TAMING THE TONGUE

REFLECTION

Begin your study by sharing thoughts on this question.

1. Why does a compliment give someone confidence?

_____

_____

_____

BIBLE READING

Read James 3:1–12 from the NCV or the NKJV.

NCV

¹My brothers and sisters, not many of you should become teachers, because you know that we who teach will be judged more strictly. ²We all make many mistakes. If people never said anything wrong, they would be perfect and able to control their entire selves, too. ³When we put bits into the mouths of horses to make them obey us, we can control their whole bodies. ⁴Also a ship is very big, and it is pushed by strong winds. But a very small rudder controls that big ship, making it go wherever the pilot wants. ⁵It is the same with the tongue.

NKJV

¹My brethren, let not many of you become teachers, knowing that we shall receive a stricter judgment. ²For we all stumble in many things. If anyone does not stumble in word, he is a perfect man, able also to bridle the whole body. ³Indeed, we put bits in horses' mouths that they may obey us, and we turn their whole body. ⁴Look also at ships: although they are so large and are driven by fierce winds, they are turned by a very small rudder wherever the pilot desires. ⁵Even so the tongue is a little member and boasts great things.

NCV

It is a small part of the body, but it brags about great things.

A big forest fire can be started with only a little flame. ⁶And the tongue is like a fire. It is a whole world of evil among the parts of our bodies. The tongue spreads its evil through the whole body. The tongue is set on fire by hell, and it starts a fire that influences all of life. ⁷People can tame every kind of wild animal, bird, reptile, and fish, and they have tamed them, ⁸but no one can tame the tongue. It is wild and evil and full of deadly poison. ⁹We use our tongues to praise our Lord and Father, but then we curse people, whom God made like himself. ¹⁰Praises and curses come from the same mouth! My brothers and sisters, this should not happen. ¹¹Do good and bad water flow from the same spring? ¹²My brothers and sisters, can a fig tree make olives, or can a grapevine make figs? No! And a well full of salty water cannot give good water.

NKJV

See how great a forest a little fire kindles! ⁶And the tongue is a fire, a world of iniquity. The tongue is so set among our members that it defiles the whole body, and sets on fire the course of nature; and it is set on fire by hell. ⁷For every kind of beast and bird, of reptile and creature of the sea, is tamed and has been tamed by mankind. ⁸But no man can tame the tongue. It is an unruly evil, full of deadly poison. ⁹With it we bless our God and Father, and with it we curse men, who have been made in the similitude of God. ¹⁰Out of the same mouth proceed blessing and cursing. My brethren, these things ought not to be so. ¹¹Does a spring send forth fresh water and bitter from the same opening? ¹²Can a fig tree, my brethren, bear olives, or a grapevine bear figs? Thus no spring yields both salt water and fresh.

DISCOVERY

Explore the Bible reading by discussing these questions.

2. How does a person's tongue compare to a horse's bit and a ship's rudder?

3. In what ways is the tongue like fire?

_____

_____

_____

4. Explain how the tongue can be used for both good and evil.

_____

_____

_____

5. Why is the tongue so difficult to control?

_____

_____

_____

6. List the examples from nature that James uses to teach the power of words.

_____

_____

_____

INSPIRATION

Here is an uplifting thought from the *Inspirational Study Bible.*

Each of us has a tongue and a voice. These instruments of speech can be used destructively or employed constructively. I can use my tongue to slander, to gripe, to scold, to nag, and to quarrel; or I can bring it under the control of God's Spirit and make it an instrument of blessing and praise. . . . Only God can control it, as we yield it to Him.

The twentieth-century version of James 3:3 says, "When we put bits into the horses' mouths to make them obey us, we control the rest of their bodies also." Just so, when we submit to the claims of Christ upon our lives, our untamed natures are brought under His control. We become meek, tamed, and "fit for the Master's service."

(from *The Secret of Happiness*
by Billy Graham)

RESPONSE

Use these questions to share more deeply with each other.

7. What are some examples of an untamed tongue?

_____

_____

_____

8. How can a person's tongue hinder his or her Christian service?

_____

_____

_____

9. How can we submit our tongues to the control of God's Spirit? What is the result?

_____

_____

_____

PRAYER

Father, change us from the inside out. Purify our hearts so that our speech will be pleasing to you. Keep us from using our words to manipulate and hurt others. Empower us by your Holy Spirit to use our tongues to sing your praises and to build others up in the faith.

JOURNALING

Take a few moments to record your personal insights from this lesson.

What can I do to let God control the words I say?

ADDITIONAL QUESTIONS

10. In what ways can our words encourage others or hurt others?

_____

_____

_____

11. What can you do to use only encouraging words?

_____

_____

_____

12. How can you speak words of blessing today?

_____

_____

_____

For more Bible passages on controlling the tongue, see Psalm 34:13; Proverbs 13:3; 21:23; Titus 3:2; James 1:26; 1 Peter 3:10.

To complete the book of James during this twelve-part study, read James 3:1–12.

ADDITIONAL THOUGHTS

LESSON SEVEN

SOWING SEEDS OF PEACE

REFLECTION

Begin your study by sharing thoughts on this question.

1. Think of a time when you saw someone bring peace to a volatile situation. How did that person bring peace?

_____

_____

_____

BIBLE READING

Read James 3:13–18 from the NCV or the NKJV

NCV

¹³Are there those among you who are truly wise and understanding? Then they should show it by living right and doing good things with a gentleness that comes from wisdom. ¹⁴But if you are selfish and have bitter jealousy in your hearts, do not brag. Your bragging is a lie that hides the truth. ¹⁵That kind of "wisdom" does not come from God but from the world. It is not spiritual; it is from the devil. ¹⁶Where jealousy and selfishness are, there will be

NKJV

¹³Who is wise and understanding among you? Let him show by good conduct that his works are done in the meekness of wisdom. ¹⁴But if you have bitter envy and self-seeking in your hearts, do not boast and lie against the truth. ¹⁵This wisdom does not descend from above, but is earthly, sensual, demonic. ¹⁶For where envy and self-seeking exist, confusion and every evil thing are there. ¹⁷But the wisdom that is from above is first pure, then peaceable,

NCV

confusion and every kind of evil. ¹⁷But the wisdom that comes from God is first of all pure, then peaceful, gentle, and easy to please. This wisdom is always ready to help those who are troubled and to do good for others. It is always fair and honest. ¹⁸People who work for peace in a peaceful way plant a good crop of right-living.

NKJV

gentle, willing to yield, full of mercy and good fruits, without partiality and without hypocrisy. ¹⁸Now the fruit of righteousness is sown in peace by those who make peace.

DISCOVERY

Explore the Bible reading by discussing these questions.

2. How would you describe "worldly wisdom"?

_____

_____

_____

3. How does Scripture describe God's wisdom?

_____

_____

_____

4. Why do jealousy and selfishness cause confusion and evil things?

_____

_____

_____

5. List some things that God's wisdom motivates people to do.

_____

_____

_____

6. What happens when people work for peace?

_____

_____

_____

INSPIRATION

Here is an uplifting thought from the *Inspirational Study Bible.*

"Those who are peacemakers will plant seeds of peace and reap a harvest of goodness."

The principle for peace is the same as the principle for crops: Never underestimate the power of a seed.

The story of Heinz is a good example. Europe, 1934. Hitler's plague of anti-Semitism was infecting a continent. Some would escape it. Some would die from it. But eleven-year-old Heinz would learn from it. He would learn the power of sowing seeds of peace.

Heinz was a Jew.

The Bavarian village of Furth, where Heinz lived, was being overrun by Hitler's young thugs. Heinz's father, a schoolteacher, lost his job. Recreational activities ceased. Tension mounted on the streets.

The Jewish families clutched the traditions that held them together—the observance of the Sabbath, of Rosh Hashanah, of Yom Kippur. Old ways took on new significance. As the clouds of persecution swelled and blackened, these ancient precepts were a precious cleft in a mighty rock.

And as the streets became a battleground, such security meant survival.

Hitler youth roamed the neighborhoods looking for trouble. Young Heinz learned to keep his eyes open. When he saw a band of troublemakers, he would step to the other side of the street. Sometimes he would escape a fight—sometimes not.

One day, in 1934, a pivotal confrontation occurred. Heinz found himself face-to-face with a Hitler bully. A beating appeared inevitable. This time, however, he walked away unhurt—not because of what he did, but because of what he said. He didn't fight back; he spoke up. He convinced the troublemakers that a fight was not necessary. His words kept battle at bay. And Heinz saw firsthand how the tongue can create peace.

He learned the skill of using words to avoid conflict. And for a young Jew in Hitler-ridden Europe, that skill had many opportunities to be honed.

Fortunately, Heinz's family escaped from Bavaria and made their way to America. Later in life, he would downplay the impact those adolescent experiences had on his development.

But one has to wonder. For after Heinz grew up, his name became synonymous with peace negotiations. His legacy became that of a bridgebuilder. Somewhere he had learned the power of the properly placed word of peace. And one has to wonder if his training didn't come on the streets of Bavaria.

You don't know him as Heinz. You know him by his Anglicized name, Henry. Henry Kissinger.

Never underestimate the power of a seed.

(from *The Applause of Heaven*
by Max Lucado)

RESPONSE

Use these questions to share more deeply with each other.

7. How does a wise person resolve conflict?

_____

_____

_____

8. What do you think it means to sow seeds of peace?

_____

_____

_____

9. Why are people sometimes unwilling to work for peace?

_____

_____

_____

PRAYER

Father, we don't always want to seek peace. Forgive us. Keep us from contributing to conflict instead of resolving it, for fanning flames of discord instead of spreading peace. Give us your wisdom, Father—wisdom to be submissive, merciful, and gentle.

JOURNALING

Take a few moments to record your personal insights from this lesson.

How can I bring peace to conflict at home, work, school, or church?

ADDITIONAL QUESTIONS

10. How does this passage challenge you to deal with conflicts in your relationships?

_____

_____

_____

11. Why is it important for Christians to sow seeds of peace?

_____

_____

_____

12. List some practical ways you can bring peace to a conflict.

_____

_____

_____

For more Bible passages on wisdom and peace, see Psalm 29:11; 34:14; 119:165; Proverbs 2:6; 3:13; 4:7; Daniel 12:3; John 14:27; Romans 8:6; Philippians 4:7; Colossians 2:2, 3.

To complete the book of James during this twelve-part study, read James 3:13–18.

ADDITIONAL THOUGHTS

LESSON EIGHT

TRUSTING GOD

REFLECTION

Begin your study by sharing thoughts on this question.

1. Would you change the way you are living if you could see your future? Why or why not?

_____

_____

_____

BIBLE READING

Read James 4:1–10 from the NCV or the NKJV.

NCV

¹Do you know where your fights and arguments come from? They come from the selfish desires that war within you. ²You want things, but you do not have them. So you are ready to kill and are jealous of other people, but you still cannot get what you want. So you argue and fight. You do not get what you want, because you do not ask God. ³Or when you ask, you do not receive because the reason you ask is wrong. You want things so you can use them for your own pleasures.

NKJV

¹Where do wars and fights come from among you? Do they not come from your desires for pleasure that war in your members? ²You lust and do not have. You murder and covet and cannot obtain. You fight and war. Yet you do not have because you do not ask. ³You ask and do not receive, because you ask amiss, that you may spend it on your pleasures. ⁴Adulterers and adulteresses! Do you not know that friendship with the world is enmity with God? Whoever therefore wants to be a friend of the

NCV

[4]So, you are not loyal to God! You should know that loving the world is the same as hating God. Anyone who wants to be a friend of the world becomes God's enemy. [5]Do you think the Scripture means nothing that says, "The Spirit that God made to live in us wants us for himself alone." [6]But God gives us even more grace, as the Scripture says,

"God is against the proud,
but he gives grace to the humble."

[7]So give yourselves completely to God. Stand against the devil, and the devil will run from you. [8]Come near to God, and God will come near to you. You sinners, clean sin out of your lives. You who are trying to follow God and the world at the same time, make your thinking pure. [9]Be sad, cry, and weep! Change your laughter into crying and your joy into sadness. [10]Don't be too proud in the Lord's presence, and he will make you great.

NKJV

world makes himself an enemy of God. [5]Or do you think that the Scripture says in vain, "The Spirit who dwells in us yearns jealously"?
[6]But He gives more grace. Therefore He says:

"God resists the proud,
But gives grace to the humble."

[7]Therefore submit to God. Resist the devil and he will flee from you. [8]Draw near to God and He will draw near to you. Cleanse your hands, you sinners; and purify your hearts, you double-minded. [9]Lament and mourn and weep! Let your laughter be turned to mourning and your joy to gloom. [10]Humble yourselves in the sight of the Lord, and He will lift you up.

DISCOVERY

Explore the Bible reading by discussing these questions.

2. What does the Bible mean when it says a war is waging inside of us?

_____

_____

_____

3. What happens when we stand against the devil?

_____

_____

_____

4. How can we stand against the devil?

_____

_____

_____

5. What promise is given to those who draw near to God?

_____

_____

_____

6. Why should people humble themselves before God?

_____

_____

_____

INSPIRATION

Here is an uplifting thought from the *Inspirational Study Bible*.

In order to know God's will there must be a willingness to do it.

Imagine a door in the path ahead of us. God's will is on the other side of that door. We crave to know what that is. Will God show us what's on the other side of that door? No. Why not? Because we have to resolve an issue on this side of the door first. If He is Lord, He has the right to determine what's on the other side of the door. If we don't afford Him that right, then we are not acknowledging Him as Lord.

Why do we want to know what's on the other side of the door? Isn't it because we want to reserve the right to determine whether or not we will go through it? Some boldly walk halfway through, but keep their foot in the door just in case they don't like what they see and want to go back. It's going to be awfully hard to continue walking with God if your foot is stuck in the door. Jesus said, "No one putting his hand to the plow and looking back is fit for the kingdom of God" (Luke 9:62).

One man probably spoke for many when he said, "I'm so used to running my own life. I'm not sure I even can or want to trust someone else. Besides, God would probably haul me off to some mission field I can't stand." What we need to realize is that if we did give our heart to the Lord, and God did call us to that mission field, by the time we got there we wouldn't want to be anywhere else.

Do you believe that the will of God is good, acceptable and perfect for you? That's the heart of the issue.

(from *Walking in the Light*
by Neil Anderson)

RESPONSE

Use these questions to share more deeply with each other.

7. Why can we trust God's will for our lives?

_____

_____

_____

8. How can people know whether they are following God's will?

_____

_____

_____

9. When have you been convinced that you knew God's will for you? What convinced you?

_____

_____

_____

PRAYER

Father, help us renew our commitment to you—to release all that we have and all that we are to you. We long to give ourselves completely to you so that we might know the freedom available to us only through your grace.

JOURNALING

Take a few moments to record your personal insights from this lesson.

How am I living my life to demonstrate my trust in God?

ADDITIONAL QUESTIONS

10. List areas of your life that are difficult for you to turn over to God's control.

_____

_____

_____

11. What truth in this lesson encourages you to trust God more fully?

_____

_____

_____

12. What steps can you take to release every part of your life to God?

_____

_____

_____

For more Bible passages on trusting God, see Psalms 62:8; 143:8; Proverbs 29:25; Isaiah 25:9; Nahum 1:7; Romans 10:11.

To complete the book of James during this twelve-part study, read James 4:1–10.

ADDITIONAL THOUGHTS

LESSON NINE

THE DANGERS OF PRIDE

REFLECTION

Begin your study by sharing thoughts on this question.

1. What is one of your long-range goals? How would you feel if you could not accomplish it?

_____

_____

_____

BIBLE READING

Read James 4:11–17 from the NCV or the NKJV.

<table>
<tr><th>NCV</th><th>NKJV</th></tr>
<tr><td>

[11]Brothers and sisters, do not tell evil lies about each other. If you speak against your fellow believers or judge them, you are judging and speaking against the law they follow. And when you are judging the law, you are no longer a follower of the law. You have become a judge. [12]God is the only Lawmaker and Judge. He is the only One who can save and destroy. So it is not right for you to judge your neighbor.

[13]Some of you say, "Today or tomorrow we will go to some city. We will stay there a year,

</td><td>

[11]Do not speak evil of one another, brethren. He who speaks evil of a brother and judges his brother, speaks evil of the law and judges the law. But if you judge the law, you are not a doer of the law but a judge. [12]There is one Lawgiver, who is able to save and to destroy. Who are you to judge another?

[13]Come now, you who say, "Today or tomorrow we will go to such and such a city, spend a year there, buy and sell, and make a profit"; [14]whereas you do not know what will happen

</td></tr>
</table>

NCV

do business, and make money." [14]But you do not know what will happen tomorrow! Your life is like a mist. You can see it for a short time, but then it goes away. [15]So you should say, "If the Lord wants, we will live and do this or that." [16]But now you are proud and you brag. All of this bragging is wrong. [17]Anyone who knows the right thing to do, but does not do it, is sinning.

NKJV

tomorrow. For what is your life? It is even a vapor that appears for a little time and then vanishes away. [15]Instead you ought to say, "If the Lord wills, we shall live and do this or that." [16]But now you boast in your arrogance. All such boasting is evil.

[17]Therefore, to him who knows to do good and does not do it, to him it is sin.

DISCOVERY

Explore the Bible reading by discussing these questions.

2. Why should we not speak against fellow Christians?

_____

_____

_____

3. In what ways do we judge others?

_____

_____

_____

4. Why do we need to keep our plans submissive to God's will?

_____

_____

_____

5. What attitude does God want us to have about the future? Why?

_____

_____

_____

6. Why is God not satisfied that we simply *know* to do good?

_____

_____

_____

INSPIRATION

Here is an uplifting thought from the *Inspirational Study Bible.*

A prison of pride is filled with self-made men and women determined to pull themselves up by their own bootstraps even if they land on their rear ends. It doesn't matter what they did or to whom they did it, or where they end up; it only matters that "I did it my way."

You've seen the prisoners. You've seen the alcoholic who won't admit his drinking problem. You've seen the woman who refuses to talk to anyone about her fears. You've seen the businessman who adamantly rejects help, even when his dreams are falling apart.

Perhaps to see such a prisoner all you have to do is look in the mirror.

"If we confess our sins . . ." The biggest word in Scriptures just might be that two letter one, if. For confessing sins—admitting failure—is exactly what prisoners of pride refuse to do.

"Well, I may not be perfect, but I'm better than Hitler and certainly kinder than Idi Amin!"

"Me a sinner? Oh, sure, I get rowdy every so often, but I'm a pretty good ol' boy."

"Listen, I'm just as good as the next guy. I pay my taxes. I coach the Little League team. I even make donations to Red Cross. Why, God's probably proud to have someone like me on his team."

Justification. Rationalization. Comparison. These are the tools of the jailbird. They sound good. They sound familiar. They even sound American. But in the kingdom, they sound hollow. . . .

When you get to the point of sorrow for your sins, when you admit that you have no other option but to cast all your cares on him, and when there is truly no other one that you can call, then cast all your cares on him, for he is waiting.

(from *The Applause of Heaven* by Max Lucado)

RESPONSE

Use these questions to share more deeply with each other.

7. How does pride deceive and destroy people?

_____

_____

_____

8. Why is humility harder to practice than pride?

_____

_____

_____

9. Who do you know who demonstrates a spirit of humility? What have you learned from that person?

_____

_____

_____

PRAYER

Father, forgive us for living for ourselves, for thinking that we don't need you. God, help us to embrace humility. Help us to remember that we can do nothing without you because you are the source of everything.

JOURNALING

Take a few moments to record your personal insights from this lesson.

How am I encouraged to know that God controls my future?

ADDITIONAL QUESTIONS

10. How has pride damaged your relationship with God or others?

_____

_____

_____

11. How can you begin to bring healing to those relationships?

_____

_____

_____

12. What steps can you take to develop a spirit of humility?

_____

_____

_____

For more Bible passages on pride, see Proverbs 11:2; 13:10; 16:5, 18; Romans 12:16; 1 Peter 5:5.

To complete the book of James during this twelve-part study, read James 4:11–17.

ADDITIONAL THOUGHTS

LESSON TEN

WARNINGS TO THE RICH

REFLECTION

Begin your study by sharing thoughts on this question.

1. Think of a time when you were blessed by the generosity of a fellow believer. How did that affect your life?

_____

_____

_____

BIBLE READING

Read James 5:1–6 from the NCV or the NKJV.

NCV

¹You rich people, listen! Cry and be very sad because of the troubles that are coming to you. ²Your riches have rotted, and your clothes have been eaten by moths. ³Your gold and silver have rusted, and that rust will be a proof that you were wrong. It will eat your bodies like fire. You saved your treasure for the last days. ⁴The pay you did not give the workers who mowed your fields cries out against you, and the cries of the workers have been heard by the Lord All-Powerful. ⁵Your life on earth was full of rich

NKJV

¹Come now, you rich, weep and howl for your miseries that are coming upon you! ²Your riches are corrupted, and your garments are moth-eaten. ³Your gold and silver are corroded, and their corrosion will be a witness against you and will eat your flesh like fire. You have heaped up treasure in the last days. ⁴Indeed the wages of the laborers who mowed your fields, which you kept back by fraud, cry out; and the cries of the reapers have reached the ears of the Lord of Sabaoth. ⁵You have lived on the earth

NCV

living and pleasing yourselves with everything you wanted. You made yourselves fat, like an animal ready to be killed. ⁶You have judged guilty and then murdered innocent people, who were not against you.

NKJV

in pleasure and luxury; you have fattened your hearts as in a day of slaughter. ⁶You have condemned, you have murdered the just; he does not resist you.

DISCOVERY

Explore the Bible reading by discussing these questions.

2. In what ways do people oppress others for personal gain?

_____

_____

_____

3. List some ungodly attitudes that cause oppression.

_____

_____

_____

4. Why does God hear the cries of the oppressed?

_____

_____

_____

5. How does God respond to the oppressed?

_____

_____

_____

6. What results from self-indulgence?

_____

_____

_____

INSPIRATION

Here is an uplifting thought from the *Inspirational Study Bible.*

We live at one of the great turning points in history. The present division of the World's resources dare not continue. And it will not. Either courageous pioneers will persuade reluctant nations to share the good earth's bounty, or we will enter an era of catastrophic conflict.

Christians should be in the vanguard. The church of Jesus Christ is the most universal body in the world today. All we need to do is truly obey the One we rightly worship. But to obey will mean to follow. And He lives among the poor and oppressed, seeking justice for those in agony. In our time, following in his steps will mean more simple personal lifestyles. It will mean transformed churches . . . costly commitment to structural change in secular society.

Do Christians today have that kind of faith and courage? Will we pioneer new models of sharing for our interdependent world? Will we dare to become the vanguard in the struggle for structural change? . . .

I am not pessimistic. God regularly accomplishes his will through faithful remnants. Even in affluent nations, there are millions of Christians who love their Lord Jesus more than houses and lands. More and more Christians are coming to realize that their Lord calls them to feed the hungry and seek justice for the oppressed.

If at this moment in history a few million Christians in affluent nations dare to join hands with the poor around the world, we will decisively influence the course of world history. Together we will strive to be a biblical people ready to follow wherever Scripture leads. We must pray for the courage to bear any cross, suffer any loss, and joyfully embrace any sacrifice that biblical faith requires in an Age of Hunger.

(from *Rich Christians in an Age of Hunger* by Ronald Sider)

RESPONSE

Use these questions to share more deeply with each other.

7. List some of the negative effects that increased wealth can have on people's lives.

_____

_____

_____

8. How should Christians view wealth?

_____

_____

_____

9. How can you use your financial resources for God's glory?

_____

_____

_____

PRAYER

Father, keep us from being so blinded by earthly possessions that we fail to see the eternal treasure we cannot lose. Forgive us when we have worked for greed and gain. Thank you for the blessing of work and for the strength to do it for you.

JOURNALING

Take a few moments to record your personal insights from this lesson.

How content am I with my financial situation?

ADDITIONAL QUESTIONS

10. How can money keep you from doing God's work?

_____

_____

_____

11. In what ways do you need to change your attitudes about money?

_____

_____

_____

12. How can you use money to accumulate treasure in heaven?

_____

_____

_____

For more Bible passages on warnings to the rich, see Proverbs 11:28; 23:4; Matthew 19:23, 24; Luke 6:24; 1 Timothy 6:9, 10; 17–19.

To complete the book of James during this twelve-part study, read James 5:1–6.

ADDITIONAL THOUGHTS

LESSON ELEVEN

THE REWARDS OF PERSEVERANCE

REFLECTION

Begin your study by sharing thoughts on this question.

1. Think of a time when you persevered in spite of difficult circumstances. What were the rewards for your perseverance?

_____

_____

_____

BIBLE READING

Read James 5:7–11 from the NCV or the NKJV.

NCV

⁷Brothers and sisters, be patient until the Lord comes again. A farmer patiently waits for his valuable crop to grow from the earth and for it to receive the autumn and spring rains. ⁸You, too, must be patient. Do not give up hope, because the Lord is coming soon. ⁹Brothers and sisters, do not complain against each other or you will be judged guilty. And the Judge is ready to come! ¹⁰Brothers and sisters, follow the example of the prophets who spoke for the Lord.

NKJV

⁷Therefore be patient, brethren, until the coming of the Lord. See how the farmer waits for the precious fruit of the earth, waiting patiently for it until it receives the early and latter rain. ⁸You also be patient. Establish your hearts, for the coming of the Lord is at hand.

⁹Do not grumble against one another, brethren, lest you be condemned. Behold, the Judge is standing at the door! ¹⁰My brethren, take the prophets, who spoke in the name of the Lord,

NCV	NKJV
They suffered many hard things, but they were patient. ¹¹We say they are happy because they did not give up. You have heard about Job's patience, and you know the Lord's purpose for him in the end. You know the Lord is full of mercy and is kind.	as an example of suffering and patience. ¹¹Indeed we count them blessed who endure. You have heard of the perseverance of Job and seen the end intended by the Lord—that the Lord is very compassionate and merciful.

DISCOVERY

Explore the Bible reading by discussing these questions.

2. Why should believers be motivated to patiently endure?

_____

_____

_____

3. How does the illustration of a farmer show the importance of patience?

_____

_____

_____

4. Whose example should believers follow? Why?

_____

_____

_____

5. What did the prophets gain from their suffering?

_____

_____

_____

6. How was God's compassion and mercy extended to Job?

_____

_____

_____

INSPIRATION

Here is an uplifting thought from the *Inspirational Study Bible.*

Bart decided to ask God to shape his character. He surrendered his own will to the will of God. At the time, Bart's business floundered on the verge of failure. "Should I throw in the towel, or keep trying to hang on?" Bart wondered.

God replies, "You need to persevere." After we have done the will of God, then we will receive our reward. God's will is for us to demonstrate to a hurting world how wonderfully His power can work within the person who perseveres.

Certainly, there are days when we feel like we will die, or maybe even wish we could, but we keep going. Why? Why do we keep going? Because *when* we have done the will of God we *will* receive what He has promised.

Will persevering guarantee we will succeed in the worldly sense of success? Is that what He has promised? Does it mean we will not go out of business if we hang on? No, but we can state emphatically that if we don't persevere we will not succeed in any sense. Not persevering guarantees we will fail. . . .

Beyond succeeding in a worldly sense though, God wants our character to succeed more than our circumstances to succeed. He will adjust our circumstances in such a way that our character eventually succeeds, for that is His highest aim, His will.

(from *Walking with Christ in the Details of Life* by Patrick Morley)

RESPONSE

Use these questions to share more deeply with each other.

7. When has it been difficult for you to persevere in your Christian walk?

_____

_____

_____

8. How have Christian friends encouraged you to persevere?

_____

_____

_____

9. What can believers do to help one another develop patience and perseverance?

_____

_____

_____

PRAYER

Father, you never promised us that this world would be easy, you never said there would be no pain. But you did promise that if we persevere, we would be blessed by your mercy and your grace. Teach us to hold firmly to your promises, so that we can endure the struggles and storms of this world.

JOURNALING

Take a few moments to record your personal insights from this lesson.

How can the promise of Christ's return help me face my daily struggles?

ADDITIONAL QUESTIONS

10. What new insight about God's character have you gained from this lesson?

_____

_____

_____

11. How does your understanding of God encourage you to persevere?

_____

_____

_____

12. How can you encourage others to persevere?

_____

_____

_____

For more Bible passages on perseverance, see Romans 2:7; 5:3, 4; 8:24, 25; 1 Timothy 4:16; Hebrews 10:36; 12:1; James 1:2–4, 12; 2 Peter 1:5–9.

To complete the book of James during this twelve-part study, read James 5:7–11.

LESSON TWELVE

PRAYERS OF FAITH

REFLECTION

Begin your study by sharing thoughts on this question.

1. Think of a time when God answered a specific prayer for you. How did that answered prayer change your life?

_____

_____

_____

BIBLE READING

Read James 5:12–20 from the NCV or the NKJV.

NCV

¹²My brothers and sisters, above all, do not use an oath when you make a promise. Don't use the name of heaven, earth, or anything else to prove what you say. When you mean yes, say only yes, and when you mean no, say only no so you will not be judged guilty.

¹³Anyone who is having troubles should pray. Anyone who is happy should sing praises. ¹⁴Anyone who is sick should call the church's elders. They should pray for and pour oil on the

NKJV

¹²But above all, my brethren, do not swear, either by heaven or by earth or with any other oath. But let your "Yes," be "Yes," and your "No," "No," lest you fall into judgment.

¹³Is anyone among you suffering? Let him pray. Is anyone cheerful? Let him sing psalms. ¹⁴Is anyone among you sick? Let him call for the elders of the church, and let them pray over him, anointing him with oil in the name of the Lord. ¹⁵And the prayer of faith will save the sick,

NCV

person in the name of the Lord. [15]And the prayer that is said with faith will make the sick person well; the Lord will heal that person. And if the person has sinned, the sins will be forgiven. [16]Confess your sins to each other and pray for each other so God can heal you. When a believing person prays, great things happen. [17]Elijah was a human being just like us. He prayed that it would not rain, and it did not rain on the land for three and a half years! [18]Then Elijah prayed again, and the rain came down from the sky, and the land produced crops again.

[19]My brothers and sisters, if one of you wanders away from the truth, and someone helps that person come back, [20]remember this: Anyone who brings a sinner back from the wrong way will save that sinner's soul from death and will cause many sins to be forgiven.

NKJV

and the Lord will raise him up. And if he has committed sins, he will be forgiven. [16]Confess your trespasses to one another, and pray for one another, that you may be healed. The effective, fervent prayer of a righteous man avails much. [17]Elijah was a man with a nature like ours, and he prayed earnestly that it would not rain; and it did not rain on the land for three years and six months. [18]And he prayed again, and the heaven gave rain, and the earth produced its fruit.

[19]Brethren, if anyone among you wanders from the truth, and someone turns him back, [20]let him know that he who turns a sinner from the error of his way will save a soul from death and cover a multitude of sins.

DISCOVERY

Explore the Bible reading by discussing these questions.

2. What advice did James give to the troubled, the cheerful, and the sick?

_____

_____

_____

3. How does prayer make a difference in the lives of believers?

_____

_____

_____

4. What steps should believers take to receive God's healing?

_____

_____

_____

5. What kind of prayer makes great things happen?

_____

_____

_____

6. What does Elijah's experience teach believers about prayer?

_____

_____

_____

INSPIRATION

Here is an uplifting thought from the *Inspirational Study Bible*.

No matter where we are, God is as close as a prayer. He is our support and strength. He will help us make our way up again from whatever depths we have fallen.

We don't often consider that sometimes Jesus is our strength simply to sit still. "Be still, and know that I am God" (Psalm 46:10). Our natural tendency when we have a painful happening in our lives is to go into action—do something. Sometimes it is wiser to wait and just be still. The answers will come.

. . . We may be sure that God is true to His word and answers all sincere prayers offered in the name of the Lord Jesus Christ. His answer may be yes, or it may be no, or it may be "Wait." If it is no or "Wait," we cannot say that God has not answered our prayer. It simply means that the answer is different from what we expected.

When we pray for help in trouble, or for healing in sickness, or for deliverance in persecution, God may not give us what we ask for because that may not be His wise and loving will for us. He will answer our prayer in His own way, and He will not let us down in our hour of need.

(from *Hope for the Troubled Heart*
by Billy Graham)

RESPONSE

Use these questions to share more deeply with each other.

7. What keeps people from turning to God in prayer?

_____

_____

_____

8. When has it been difficult for you to accept God's answer to your prayer?

_____

_____

_____

9. How can you develop more discipline and patience in your prayer life?

_____

_____

_____

PRAYER

Father, we cherish your promise to answer our prayers. And yet we often come to you with muddled ideas, unsure of what is best, uncertain of your will, and unwilling to wait patiently for your answers. We thank you, Father, for the assurance that our imperfect prayers cannot hinder your incredible power.

JOURNALING

Take a few moments to record your personal insights from this lesson.

Write a prayer to God about a situation that is troubling you.

ADDITIONAL QUESTIONS

10. What great things would you like to see God do in your life or the lives of others?

_____

_____

_____

11. What commitment are you willing to make to pray for those things?

_____

_____

_____

12. Who can keep you accountable to follow through on your commitment?

_____

_____

_____

For more Bible passages on prayer, see Psalm 6:9; Proverbs 15:8, 29; Matthew 21:22; Philippians 4:6, 7; Colossians 4:2; 1 Peter 3:12.

To complete the book of James during this twelve-part study, read James 5:12–20.

ADDITIONAL THOUGHTS

ADDITIONAL THOUGHTS

ADDITIONAL THOUGHTS

LEADERS' NOTES

LESSON ONE

Question 2: These related passages may contribute to the group's discussion on trials: 2 Corinthians 4:16–18; 2 Thessalonians 1:3, 4; Hebrews 12:2–13; 1 Peter 4:12–19; Revelation 2:3.

Question 4: Some members of your group may be facing difficult problems. This question will encourage them to ask God for wisdom. Remind them of Jesus' promise in Matthew 21:22.

LESSON TWO

Question 3: Scripture promises good things to those who remain faithful through temptation: See Matthew 10:22; Luke 21:19; 1 Corinthians 1:8; 15:58; 1 Peter 5:8–10.

Question 4: Some people try to lessen the guilt of their own sin by blaming God for tempting them. But Scripture teaches that God never tempts people to sin. Rather than blaming God for our mistakes, we need to accept responsibility, repent, and seek forgiveness.

Question 8 and 9: God did not create people to be completley independent creatures. He wants people to depend on one another for mutual support. The body of Christ functions best when believers encourage, comfort, admonish, challenge, and help each other. See Acts 4:32–35; Romans 12:4–8; Galatians 6:10; Ephesians 5:19–21.

LESSON THREE

Question 5: Read Exodus 15:26; Deuteronomy 32:45–47; and 2 Chronicles 14:2–6.

Question 9: Ask a group member to read aloud Ephesians 6:10–18. Discuss how we can use the armor of God to protect ourselves from the world's influence.

LESSON FOUR

Question 1: You may wish to ask this question again at the end of your lesson. If so, take the opportunity to develop a strategy on what the members of your group can do to make people feel welcome.

LESSON FIVE

Question 6: Prepare yourself before class by reading the story of Abraham (Genesis 12–24) and the story of Rahab (Joshua 2 and 6).

Question 10: Your class may want to apply this lesson by doing a service project as a group. Consider opportunities in your church, a nearby shelter, or another ministry.

LESSON SIX

Question 4: Look up selected proverbs on the tongue: Proverbs 6:17; 10:20; 15:4; 18:21.

Question 11: Encourage your class to hold each other accountable in the way they speak. Other close friends or family members can also help us improve our speech.

LESSON SEVEN

Question 3: You may wish to look up other verses that describe God's wisdom: 1 Corinthians 1:21–24; Colossians 2:2, 3; Revelation 5:12.

Question 11: Other places in the Bible talk about peace and peacemakers. Look up Psalm 34:14; 37:37; Proverbs 16:14; Matthew 5:9; 5:24.

LESSON EIGHT

Question 3: Share this quote from a Christian teacher named Hermas who lived around 150 A.D: "[The devil] cannot dominate the servants of God who hope in him with all their hearts. The devil can wrestle, but he cannot pin. If, then, you resist him, he will flee defeated from you in disgrace."

Question 4: Show your group that they can resist the devil by: 1. Remembering God never leaves them (Romans 8:38–39); 2. Refusing to live in guilt (1 John 1:9); 3. Praying often (1 Thessalonians 5:16–24).

LESSON NINE

Question 4: Remind your group that although we may make plans, only God knows what the future holds. See Proverbs 27:1; Luke 12:16–21.

Question 7: You can illustrate this point by taking time to read the story of King Nebuchad-nezzar in Daniel 4.

LESSON TEN

Question 1: One way your group can apply this lesson is to take a collection for someone else in your church who is struggling financially. Consider giving money or a bag of groceries to someone in need.

Question 7: Look up other portions of Scripture that speak about the negative effects wealth can have. See Exodus 20:17; Proverbs 18:11; Luke 18:24; 1 Timothy 6:9–10.

Question 9: See also Proverbs 11:24, 25; 19:17; 20:10, 23; 21:13; 28:2; Malachi 3:8–10; Luke 12:33–34; Romans 13:6–7.

LESSON ELEVEN

Question 5: Look up Old Testament references that tell about prophets who suffered: Exodus 17:1–7; 1 Kings 18:3, 4; 18:10–19:2; 2 Kings 6:31; 2 Chronicles 18:12–27; 24:20–22; Jeremiah 37:1–38:13; Daniel 6.

LESSON TWELVE

Question 2: Other passages encourage followers of God to pray if they are in trouble. See Psalms 30; 50:15; 91:15.

Question 6: If you have the time, read excerpts from Elijah's story found in 1 Kings 17:1–18:46.

ADDITIONAL NOTES

ADDITIONAL NOTES

ADDITIONAL NOTES

ADDITIONAL NOTES

ADDITIONAL NOTES

ADDITIONAL NOTES

ADDITIONAL NOTES

ADDITIONAL NOTES

ADDITIONAL NOTES

ADDITIONAL NOTES

ADDITIONAL NOTES

ACKNOWLEDGMENTS

Anderson, Neil. *Walking in the Light*, copyright 1984 by Thomas Nelson, Nashville, Tennessee.

Graham, Billy. *The Holy Spirit*, copyright 1988, Word, Inc., Dallas, Texas.

Graham, Billy. *Hope for the Troubled Heart*, copyright 1991, Word, Inc., Dallas, Texas.

Graham, Billy. *The Secret of Happiness*, copyright 1985, Word, Inc., Dallas, Texas.

Lucado, Max. *The Applause of Heaven*, copyright 1990, Word, Inc., Dallas, Texas.

Lucado, Max. *On the Anvil*, copyright 1985 by Max Lucado. Used by permission of Tyndale House Publishers, Inc. All rights reserved.

Morley, Patrick. *Walking with Christ in the Details of Life*, copyright 1992 by Thomas Nelson, Nashville, Tennessee.

Ortlund, Anne. *My Sacrifice, His Fire*, copyright 1991, Word, Inc., Dallas, Texas.

Sider, Ronald. *Rich Christians in an Age of Hunger*, copyright 1990, Word, Inc., Dallas, Texas.

Smalley, Gary and John Trent. *A Dad's Blessing*, copyright 1994 by Thomas Nelson, Nashville, Tennessee.